CHRISTIE'S
COLLECTIBLES

4/23 $1

CHRISTIE'S
COLLECTIBLES

STAFFORDSHIRE FIGURES

Geoffrey Stafford Charles

A BULFINCH PRESS BOOK
LITTLE, BROWN AND COMPANY
BOSTON • NEW YORK • TORONTO • LONDON

First North American Edition

ISBN 0-8212-2461-1

Library of Congress Catalog Card Number 97-071295

PROJECT EDITOR THERESA LANE
PROJECT ART EDITOR HELEN SPENCER
PICTURE EDITOR ELIZABETH LOVING

Marshall Editions would like to thank
Harriet Stafford Charles for her help
in the creation of this book.

Conceived, edited, and designed by
Marshall Editions
170 Piccadilly London W1V 9DD

Bulfinch Press is an imprint and trademark of
Little, Brown and Company (Inc.)

Published simultaneously in Canada by
Little, Brown & Company (Canada) Limited

PRINTED IN PORTUGAL

CHRISTIE'S
502 Park Avenue New York NY 10022

CHRISTIE'S EAST
219 East 67th Street New York NY 10021

CHRISTIE'S CANADA
170 Bloor Street West Suite 210 Toronto Ontario M5S IT9

CHRISTIE'S
8 King Street St. James's London SW1Y 6QT

CHRISTIE'S SOUTH KENSINGTON
85 Old Brompton Road London SW7 3LD

CHRISTIE'S AUSTRALIA
180 Jersey Road Woollahra Sydney NSW 2025

CHRISTIE'S SOUTH AFRICA
P.O. Box 72126 Parkview Johannesburg 2122

CHRISTIE'S JAPAN
Sankyo Ginza Building 6-5-13 Ginza Chuo-ku Tokyo 104

Contents

PRICE CODES

The following price codes are used in this book:
$A Less than $225 **$B** $226–$600
$C $601–$1,200 **$D** $1,201–$3,750 **$E** $3,751–$11,250
$F $11,251–$22,500 **$G** More than $22,500

Valuation is an imprecise art and prices can vary for many reasons, including the condition of a piece, fashion, and national and regional interest. Prices given in this book are approximate and based on likely *auction* values. *Insurance* values reflect the retail replacement price and as such are liable to be higher.

Introduction

$\mathcal{S}$TAFFORDSHIRE FIGURES ARE AMONG THE MOST EASILY recognizable artefacts in British ceramics. Potters first made them early in the 18th century and continued until World War II, and some are reproduced to this day. They are as cherished now as they were in the 19th century. At the time, they were popular because they were cheap alternatives to the expensive and prestigious models made for the rich by the great porcelain manufacturers. Today, they are collected across the world, including in the United States, because they represent a slice of history and the charm of a bygone era.

$\mathcal{A}$lthough the work is largely perceived as models of people and, of course, the ubiquitous dogs, Staffordshire

Kilns for firing pottery, like those used in Staffordshire, are shown in this 1831 illustration by G.S. Shepherd.

This delicate Meissen figure of Columbine from c.1744 is an example of the expensive porcelain figures appreciated by the elite.

potters made a huge variety of wares, including ordinary household items such as pitchers, plates, and tea sets. Staffordshire figures are seen as a generic type, since it is rare to attribute particular pieces to individual potters. Although they were hand finished and painted, the majority of figures were made from molds, so the level of individuality is reduced. Nevertheless, the inherent fragility of any ceramic artefact makes many pieces rare; it is their rarity and the fascinating range of subject matter that make most pieces endearing and highly collectable.

The subject matter of Staffordshire figures has changed during the history of the genre, resulting in an immense selection of pieces. Early pieces are often concerned with rural or classical themes. It was later, from the 1840s on that portrait figures celebrating great events in contemporary public life became prevalent. This may have been connected to Queen Victoria's ascension to the throne and the expansion of the British Empire, along with the changing political scene in Europe. Today's equivalents would probably include models of Diana, the Princess of Wales, President Clinton, and sports heroes such as Michael Jordan. It was not only statesmen, military heroes and royalty that appealed to the potters and the public; huge numbers of models depicting theatrical and

A ballad sheet from c.1827 by H.G. Maguire for the song Buy Image! *shows a street vendor selling figures.*

notorious personalities were made as well. The theatrical groups were often copied from printed material advertising the production, and the figures were sold outside the theater. A smaller number of figures were of criminals and crime scenes. Aromatic burners, often modeled as houses, were also created – appallingly poor sanitation in the mid-19th century made such items essential to any city household.

The earliest figures are now rare, and prices dictate that the ordinary collector will be unlikely to obtain such pieces as "Polito's Menagerie" (see p.34) or a saltglaze bear pitcher (see p.13). By their very nature, fewer of these pieces have survived. Subsequent developments in pottery techniques have created more substantial and long-lasting wares. For example, the use of molds, with few – or no – applied pieces that could be broken off, made later pieces less susceptible to accidents. Naturally, age is a factor; early pieces have had to survive intact longer than mid-19th century items.

Complicated early pieces with several figures and intricate details were made by hand from sheets and strips of clay and built up in gradual stages. Single figures of animals from the late 18th century were sometimes made by "slip molding"; liquid clay, or slip, was poured into ready-made single plaster molds. Before firing, extra appendages, made by hand, were added to the form to give the figures a three-dimensional appearance. By the mid-19th century, the "flatback" figures were made almost entirely from a mold in two parts. Sheets of clay were pressed into each side of the mold, which was then drawn together; the pieces squeezed outside were cut off, leaving a ridge, or mold line. These molds were used several hundred times until the features became indistinct.

Decorating techniques also evolved. Early pieces were fired, then sparingly decorated in simple colored glazes and given a "glaze firing," that is, a second firing to fix

The evangelist Dwight Lynam Moody was made in this press mold from the Samson Smith factory.

the glaze. The later pieces were given the initial "biscuit" firing, followed by a clear glaze firing, and only then were painted with bright overglaze enamels, which were fired yet another time. Overglaze enamel decoration used ground glass within a medium of oil, which burned off during the firing process. These paints were applied in stages, because certain colors set at different temperatures. Although the mid-19th century figures used almost entirely overglaze enamels, sometimes one of the firings was omitted as a way of saving on cost. The piece was colored by using cobalt (blue) or manganese (purple), which could be painted on after the biscuit firing and fired under the clear glaze.

Although it is often difficult to ascertain which factory a figure came from, there are exceptions. Such makers as Obadiah Sherratt, Thomas Whieldon, the Wood family, and others have distinctive identifying factors – perhaps their style, a written record, or a mark. The Wood family were probably the first to use a mark – the family name impressed into the body. Sherratt's work is also easy to detect: it is well recorded, and his subject matter is peculiar to his factory. Other potters copied success-ful wares made by the more original and better-known factories.

Staffordshire potters made practical wares, such as this tea canister from c.1785, with King George III in relief.

This 1860 group of the two Cushman sisters in the roles of Romeo and Juliet was modeled on a playbill.

TIPS FOR COLLECTORS

• Buy figures you like and can afford. Don't let others pressure you into buying pieces for your collection.

• Avoid common 19th-century figures with restoration. With diligence, you should find an almost perfect piece. Many early pieces have damage, however; restoration may be unavoidable. Restoration is measured by quality: some pieces are lovingly restored, but others are rough.

• Clean pieces with care: heavy scrubbing can damage overglaze enamels. Occasional gentle cleaning in mild, soapy, lukewarm water is adequate. Because restoration work has not been fired, do not wash restored pieces.

• Try to buy from specialists or reputable auction houses, who can guide you in your purchases and look for pieces you would like to augment your collection.

• Nobody wants a fake in their collection. If you don't know what you are looking for, ask someone who does. Modern reproductions use a different pottery body, and the glaze is overly crazed to give an appearance of age.

Pew group

THIS GROUP IS AMONG THE EARLIEST RECOGNIZED
figure groups from the Staffordshire potters.
It is a typical "pew group" from c.1745, so-called
because of the way in which the figures are
seated on a pew. It is difficult to say exactly how
many survive – perhaps as few as 10. They
are in such high demand by wealthy collectors
that the pieces circulate among them
and appear at auction more often than might be
expected – but this is still infrequent.
THIS PEW GROUP IS MADE FROM SALTGLAZE POTTERY.
Handfuls of salt were thrown into the kiln during
the firing process. The salt vaporized and formed
a glaze on the surface, which has a rough,
colorless texture. In contrast to the majority of
19th-century figures, these groups are predominantly
made by modeling pieces of clay by hand.
Height 6¼in/16cm \$G

Saltglaze bear pitcher

THE EXTRUDED CLAY FUR ON THIS FIGURE MAKES
it appear to be different from the pew group
(see opposite), but it is another example of saltglaze.
At first glance, the bear may look like an ornamental
piece, but, in fact, it is a pitcher – the head
comes off and functions as a lid and drinking cup.
Decoration is limited to a sparse amount of brown
glaze to highlight the eyes, paws, and collar.
AS REFLECTED IN ITS VALUE, THIS IS ONE OF THE EARLIER
types of bear-baiting pitchers, made c.1750.
Such items were manufactured, however, in a variety
of styles and bodies well into the 19th century.
This reflects the fact that bear-baiting was a
popular sport for many years, being outlawed only
in 1835. The dog visible between the bear's
front legs is a common feature that illustrates
the role of baiting dogs in the sport.
Height 10½in/26.5cm $F

Whieldon owl pitcher

*THOMAS WHIELDON WAS FIRST APPRENTICED TO
John Astbury, one of the original known potters of
Staffordshire who made basic molded figures
decorated with simple colored glazes. By 1740,
Whieldon had his own family-run pottery in Fenton
Low, producing wares similar to those made by
Astbury. Instead of over-painting with colored
enamels, they both used colored glazes that were
created by firing metal oxides into the glaze.*

*MODELED ON A NATURALISTIC FORM, THIS CREAMWARE OWL
pitcher, made c.1760, has a removable head that
serves as a lid. The mottled glazes are often
attributed to Thomas Whieldon, but not all such
products were made by this family of potters.*

Height 6in/15cm $G

Such details as the eyebrows,
feathers, and wings were
made by applying strips of
molded clay to the body.

Arbor group

THIS ARBOR GROUP, FROM C.1765, IS MADE
*from a cream-colored earthenware known as
creamware. By the mid-18th century,
English porcelain manufacturers, such as Chelsea
and Bow, were producing a variety of figures
that were influenced by oriental and continental
designs. Some enterprising Staffordshire potters,
including John Astbury, filled a gap in the
market by using less expensive creamware to
make figures in a porcelain style.*
THE TWO WOMEN IN THE ARBOR WERE PRESS-MOLDED;
*the arbor itself was probably modeled by
hand. The piece is colored with yellow, green,
and brown glazes. These groups are very
rare, particularly ones that feature two
women. Most single figures are of men,
for example, musicians and soldiers.*
Height 5in/13cm $G

Pratt-type group

MADE OF A BUFF-COLORED POTTERY BODY, THIS group of a cow, calf, and milkmaid is known as a Pratt type, after the family of potters who worked in Lane Delft, in the Potteries area in Staffordshire. Although this particular group is thought to have been made in Yorkshire c.1800–20, not Staffordshire, the Pratt name is used generically to indicate this type of colored decoration. It was not uncommon for potters around the country to take their inspiration from the popular pieces emanating from Staffordshire, which was the largest area of pottery production in Great Britain.

THE BASE HAS AN INTERESTING SPONGE PATTERN, AND THE figure itself has unusual color schemes (the purple patches on the body of the cow, for example). This group was popular into the late 19th century, although the body and style changed by the 1850s.

Height 6in/15cm $D

Pratt-type plaques

THESE PLAQUES HAVE DISTINCTIVE PRATT-TYPE colored glazes decorating creamware or pearlware pottery bodies. They illustrate the late 18th- to early 19th-century taste for classical subjects, including (clockwise from top left): a woman, perhaps Sorrow; a woman with a winged putto, possibly Venus and Cupid; a woman holding grapes – she may be Ariadne; Prometheus chained to a rock, being attacked by an eagle; and a molded muse among acanthus leaf decoration.

THE MUSE HAS A PEARLWARE BODY, SO-CALLED BECAUSE OF the color of its glaze, which was intended to imitate porcelain and became more popular than creamware (the other plaques are creamware). Pearlware is produced by adding a small amount of cobalt to the glaze to give it a bluish, porcelaneous effect.

Height Ariadne 8in/20cm $B each

Creamware figures

*P*RATT-TYPE GLAZES WERE APPLIED TO THESE *creamware figures, dating from the late 18th to early 19th centuries. Because they were easily and inexpensively produced, figures such as these were made in vast quantities, and many have survived because they are robust. They were made by a process known as slip molding, where slip, or liquid clay, was poured into a ready-made mold, which could be used many times.*

*F*IGURES REPRESENTING THE SEASONS WERE POPULAR. *The boy holding a basket of flowers might represent summer or fall. It is not clear whether the woman holding a bundle represents any particular season or is merely intended to illustrate rural pastimes.*

Height woman 5½in/14cm $A

Pearlware classical figures

*THESE CLASSICAL FIGURES PORTRAY, FROM LEFT
to right, Cleopatra; a woman who is probably
emblematic of Love; a woman who may be Hygeia,
the goddess of health; and a figure representing
Fortitude. These pieces, made c.1800–20, are
typical of the execution of historical and
mythological figures by various Staffordshire
potters. Less typical, is the substantial size of the
two center examples, which have become
increasingly more difficult to find.*

*THE SMALLER FIGURES OF CLEOPATRA AND FORTITUDE,
which are representative of the Ralph Wood type,
are about 8in/20cm high. If in reasonable condition
and not produced by an identifiable potter,
they are worth about a tenth of the value of their
larger counterparts. The smaller figures, however,
are more likely to be available at auction.*

Height Love 29½in/75cm $D

Pearlware Rooster

FIGURES OF FARM ANIMALS AND BIRDS WERE popular into the mid-19th century. Gambling on cock fighting, a prevalent sport, was a favorite pastime of many people. From the mid-18th century, many of these figures were painted with a combination of colored glazes. This late 18th- to early 19th-century rooster, however, was painted with enamels over a pearl glaze.

COLORED ENAMELS DEMAND A GREAT DEGREE OF KNOWLEDGE to produce and apply them properly. Enamels are frit, or glass-based, paints which produce their colors upon firing. Pieces decorated with enamels need more firings than those with glazes, making them more costly. Despite this, the more brilliant enamels soon replaced the glazes.

Height 3¾in/9.5cm $B

Wood-type Neptune

THE WOODS WERE A LARGE FAMILY of potters working in Burslem at the end of the 18th century and had various partnerships between them. It is difficult to know precisely whether unmarked pieces, such as the ones here, were made by them, or by other potters who simply copied their work or who were in partnership with them. Some basic marks were used (probably by Ralph Wood II and III) and took the form of their names impressed in the body: "Ra. Wood Burslem."

These marked pieces clearly identify the type of work manufactured by the Wood family; other pieces that are similar are known generically as Wood-type.

NEPTUNE WAS A POPULAR CLASSICAL subject. These figures represent two ways the subject was handled at different periods: a pearlware Wood-type bust from the late 18th century and a creamware Wood-type Neptune standing on a dolphin, from the early 19th century.

Height bust 11½in/29cm $B–C
Height figure 11in/28cm $B

Wood-type Toby jug

THE ORIGIN OF THE TOBY JUG IS UNKNOWN, BUT it is one of the most recognizable and enduring of Staffordshire products. Some have suggested that Toby was the hero Uncle Toby of Laurence Sterne's book Tristram Shandy, *but others believe that he may have been a character by the name of Toby Philpot, a celebrated Yorkshire drinker.*

THIS LATE 18TH-CENTURY WOOD-TYPE JUG WAS MODELED in a typical seated pose, with the man holding a mug of foaming ale. Tobies come in many shapes and sizes, and in characters other than Uncle Toby, including World War I generals. The Toby featured here is slightly less common than most Wood-type examples. More common pearlware Toby jugs are worth half its value at auction; rarer types, such as Martha Gunn, could be worth double.

Height 10in/25cm $C

Figure of Chaucer

GEOFFREY CHAUCER, THE *celebrated author of* The Canterbury Tales, *is one example of the vast catalog of famous literary figures depicted by Staffordshire potters. Milton and Shakespeare are more common. The figure often stands on a marbled or mottled base, next to a pedestal topped by books on which the author leans.*

AN EARLY EXAMPLE OF *this type, dating from the late 18th to early 19th century, the figure here is decorated with an overglaze enamel. These characters continued to feature in the more readily available flatback figures of the mid-19th century. The Derby porcelain factory produced similar pedestal-type figures at the time and may be where the inspiration came from.*

Height 12½in/31.5cm $C

On the pedestal, under the book in Chaucer's hand, is a delicately shaped face. Another detail is the painted flowers on the inside of the coat.

Vicar & Moses

Vicar & Moses

ONE OF THE MOST AMUSING STAFFORDSHIRE
subjects, this group from c.1800 is an unusual one,
showing an inebriated vicar being helped home
by his clerk, Moses. (A reproduction version of this
group is shown on page 77.) More common
examples show the vicar asleep in a pulpit and
Moses attempting to wake him; these fetch half the
price of the one here at auction.

THE GROUP HAS BEEN ATTRIBUTED TO ENOCH WOOD,
who was a later member of the large Wood
family of potters of Burslem. Enoch
moved away from the family's earlier styles.
His modeling often demonstrated greater
clarity and definition, perhaps because in
his youth he studied under his uncle William
Caddick, a painter in Liverpool.

Height 11½in/29cm $C

Bocage with St. Peter

PETER

THIS 1820–30 PEARLWARE FIGURE OF ST. PETER IS completely painted in overglazed enamels. St. Peter is kneeling in prayer, with a rooster and the Gospel of St. Mark beside him. The raised pad on the front of the base, with the words "St Peter," is not unusual but neither is it the norm. Painted titles became fashionable by the mid-19th century.

LITTLE IS LEFT OF THE FOLIAGE, BUT WHAT IS THERE IS A GOOD example of a bocage. The term refers to the foliate sprig decoration and tree that often accompany such models. It was popular with porcelain manufacturers because it provided a way to support figures that might otherwise sag in the kiln during firing. Because of the nature of pottery figures, the risk of sagging is not as marked – the bocage has a purely decorative function.

Height 8½in/21.5cm $B

Walton bocage group

THIS "TENDERNESS" GROUP of a shepherd and a girl standing before a flowering bocage, with a sheep in the foreground, was made c.1825. It was made in several parts: the figures, the sheep, the foliage of the bocage, and the base were all separately molded, then applied as a whole. It is a good example of pottery from the Walton school, which often made figures with people or animals in front of a bocage. This model has a genuine mark, making it attributable to John Walton.

WALTON WORKED IN BURSLEM FROM THE LATE 18TH to early 19th centuries, but there are a number of other manufacturers who made similar wares. Identification is only possible when the potters, such as the Salt and Tittensor families, mark their pieces. Some later reproductions carry the scroll mark, so care must be taken to examine the body, coloring, and style before confirming attribution.

Height 7¾in/20cm $C

A scroll mark stamped "Walton" at the back of the figure, identifies John Walton as the maker.

Bocage with a doe

*A DOE STANDING BEFORE A FLOWERING BOCAGE
is the subject of this pearlware model, painted
with enamels, from c.1820. Deer were a popular
subject, as suggested by the many surviving
examples; this may have been because they had
sporting significance or for purely sentimental
reasons. Sheep were also a favorite.*

*SOMETIMES THE SUBJECT APPEARS NOT AS A PURELY
decorative bocage group, but as a spill vase,
frequently as a pair consisting of a stag and doe.
It is likely that this model was once part of
such a pair, and it would be reasonably easy to find
a matched mate. These naive bocage groups, with
their extensive enamel decoration, must
have been reasonably expensive to produce – but
still cheaper than a porcelain equivalent.*

Height 6½in/16.5cm $B

Bird spill

THIS UNUSUALLY ELABORATE, BUT COMPARATIVELY inexpensive, group from c.1810 depicts a pair of birds perched beside an egg-filled nest in a tree, with a group of sheep in front. It would be more typical to have either the birds or the sheep, not both. Similar bird spills continued to be made into the mid-19th century.

A SPILL VASE IS USUALLY MODELED WITH THE TRUNK of a tree, or another similarly shaped object, functioning as the holder of wooden spills (used for lighting candles, pipes and the like, much as a match is used). Due to their ornate nature, such spills were probably given as presents to a smoker or were purchased as a decorative item to sit on a mantelpiece.

Height 6in/15cm $B

Pearlware tiger group

PAINTED WITH OVERGLAZED ENAMELS, THIS
*large pearlware group is of a tiger on a stepped
base attacking a deer. Although it is similar
to other tiger groups made in the early 19th
century by Obadiah Sherratt, the potter
usually used a style of base that more closely
resembles a table. The tiger and deer group is not
very common – more typically, the tiger is
attacking an Indian army officer in a group
known as "The Death of Munroe."*
A CLOSE EXAMINATION OF THE PIECE WILL REVEAL HOW
*relatively easy it would be to change the group,
substituting the deer for Lieutenant Munroe or
vice versa. The deer itself is a separate piece
from the tiger and the base. This particular design
is illustrative of the versatile nature of many
Staffordshire figures. During this period,
the process of creating the groups might include
both molding and modeling by hand.*
Length 14½in/37cm \$F

The Dandies

THE PEARLWARE GROUP known as "The Dandies" could have been made by a number of Staffordshire manufacturers, including Obadiah Sherratt. This example is unlikely to be by Sherratt, however, since the figures are standing on a square base with no adornment. Indeed, it is Sherratt's bases that make much of his work recognizable. Sherratt's rendering of the group typically has a rocky molded base with elaborate scrolls at the front.

WHOEVER THE MANUFACTURER, ALL THE FIGURES ARE similar. They show a man and woman fashionably dressed, strolling arm-in-arm. In the 1820s, the elaborate fashions of the day must have appeared somewhat amusing to many people, and these figures may have been a humorous pastiche commenting on London vanity. It is likely that "The Dandies" was only in production for about 10 years or so; however, it still appears at auction a few times a year.

Height 8in/20cm $C

Pearlware camels

THESE PEARLWARE SPILL VASES, DESIGNED TO FACE
*each other, are modeled after two types of camels:
the bactrian and the dromedary. Because this is
an unusual subject for Staffordshire potters,
especially in 1825–30 when these figures were made,
they are more valuable than those of similar quality
of commonplace European animals.*
ALTHOUGH THE CAMELS ARE FULLY PAINTED IN OVERGLAZE
*enamels, in shades of brown for the body and green
for the base, they are drab in comparison to
other figures with an enamel finish. The modeler,
however, paid attention to detail – the hair, for
example, was incised by hand. He must have studied
a contemporary engraving because the rendering
of the camels is not nearly as naive or fanciful
as some other exotic animals, such as lions
and tigers, which were probably produced in the
late 1700s. It has been noted that in 1810, a
camel, the property of Gilbert Pidcock, was sold
as "the only one alive in England."*

Length 6in/15cm $E

Sherratt bull-baiting group

*O*BADIAH *S*HERRATT *WAS A PROLIFIC POTTER*
who worked in the Burslem area in the early 19th
century. He produced a wide variety of subjects,
and his observation and sense of the
macabre have made him a favorite Staffordshire
potter among many collectors.

*T*HIS CREAM-COLORED POTTERY GROUP, MADE
c.1820–30, is a study of bull baiting. It depicts a
chained bull tossing a terrier over one shoulder
while another terrier bites the bull's nose.
At the bull's hindquarters a man, known as Captain
Lad, stands with his arms raised. Two oval
pads, inscribed "Bull Beating" and "Now Captin
Lad" (sic), were applied on the base.

*I*N THIS, THE LARGER OF TWO GROUPS THAT *S*HERRATT
produced on the subject, the figures stand
on a table base – suitable for supporting such a
heavy body. This type of base was typically
associated with Sherratt's work.

Length 15¾in/40cm $D

Sherratt Red Barn group

*B*ASED ON A MURDER THAT WAS A CELEBRATED NEWS
*story in 1827, "The Red Barn" group (1828–30)
is an example of Sherratt's interest in topical subjects
that gripped the public imagination. William Corder
shot, stabbed, and strangled Maria Marten and
buried her under the floor of a barn. When Maria's
body was found and Corder was arrested, he
said that she had committed suicide – clearly a risible
story – but he finally confessed and was hanged
shortly afterward. This case, with its elements of
sex, violence, and wickedness, inspired a play
which, although it used a degree of artistic license,
remained popular for many years.*

*T*HIS IS A KNOWN *S*HERRATT PIECE: IT HAS HIS FAMILIAR
*table base, and his bocage is slightly different
from the bocages of other manufacturers.
Eventually, more pieces might be attributable to
other potters through the study of variations
in the leaves and flowers on bocages.*

Length 11in/28cm \$E

Polito's Menagerie

IN 1808 THE CIRCUS VISITED WOLVERHAMPTON, not far from Burslem where Sherratt was based. It is likely that Sherratt saw the circus, or a poster for it, and was inspired to create "Polito's Menagerie" (c.1825–35). Inscribed on the piece are the words: "Politos menagerie of the wonderfull burds and beasts from most part of the world: Lion&C" (sic). Wombwell, another circus owner, succeeded Polito, and later groups may be of his menagerie. MANY CONSIDER THIS GROUP TO BE SHERRATT'S MASTERPIECE. It was technically a difficult piece to fire, due to the size of the base and the applied figures (separately modeled and attached to the base), which might all have had different rates of shrinkage. It is painted in overglaze enamels, which would have required different firing temperatures for some colors. The group is possibly earlier than the date suggested, since Polito died in 1814.

Width 13¾in/35cm $F

Bust of Maria Foote

MARIA FOOTE WAS A FAMOUS AND *talented actress of the London stage in the 19th century. She also toured extensively. It was her notorious private life, however, which made her an appealing subject for Sherratt. She had many lovers and two illegitimate children. When an engagement was broken off, Maria won a breach of promise action and was awarded £3,000 in compensation – a huge amount of money at the time. Maria retired from the stage in 1831 and married the Earl of Harrington.*

THE BUST OF MARIA FOOTE, MADE C.1816, IS TYPICAL *of bust figures of the period. This one is easily identifiable as a Sherratt creation, because it rests on one of his characteristic table bases. Most other manufacturers used a socle, or pedestal, base. All the busts were painted in a similar fashion, with bright enamels. The high value of this relatively simple piece reflects both Sherratt's popularity among modern collectors and the comparative rarity of this subject.*

Height 11½in/29cm $D

Various animals

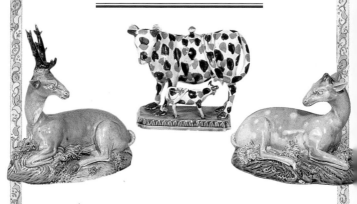

*ANIMALS WERE FAVORED BY MANY POTTERS
in the last quarter of the 18th century. This typical
selection includes a Yorkshire pearlware cow
creamer and cover (above center), a pair
of Ralph Wood-type creamware models of
a stag and hind (above left and right), and a
pair of pearlware models of a ewe and ram,
possibly from Yorkshire (below).*

*COMPARATIVELY EASY PIECES TO MANUFACTURE, THESE
figures were molded and decorated with
colored glazes. Presumably, along with the
relatively simple molded figures of people, animals
such as these would have been the mainstay
of the average Staffordshire potter of the period.
The cow creamer and cover are valued at the*

*lower end of
the price range;
the other
figures are at the
upper end of
the range.*

Length cow creamer
6½in/16.5cm $D–E

Pearlware lion

*L*IONS ARE ALWAYS A POPULAR SUBJECT WITH
*collectors and, indeed, appear to have been popular
when they were first made – there are many types
and styles produced by a variety of potters.*
*T*HIS EARLY 19TH-CENTURY PEARLWARE LION STANDS ON
*an oval stepped base, playfully resting a forepaw
on a yellow ball with black dots. The figure was
decorated in overglaze enamel. Although it
was influenced by the famous Florentine
Medici lions, this model is a comparatively naive
rendering of the subject – even for Staffordshire
pieces. Generally, the lions have greater
definition than this one does, particularly
pearlware examples from the late 18th century.
The lions were usually manufactured in pairs,
like the original Medici lions.*
Length 6¼in/16cm $D

Lloyd of Shelton-type lions

THESE LLOYD OF SHELTON-TYPE LIONS HAVE extruded clay manes and are modeled recumbent, with lambs in the foreground. Dating from c.1840, the figures are representative of lions in a biblical context. By the mid-19th century, most figures appear to have some gilding, however little. In comparison, considerable gilding was used on these examples to outline and decorate the bases and to highlight small features on the lions. Along with this more liberal use of gilding, the pottery body itself changed; it has a more porcelaneous nature.

JOHN AND REBECCA LLOYD OF SHELTON WERE KNOWN TO be working in Shelton from 1834 to 1852. They produced several figures and groups, not only in earthenware but also in porcelain, possibly reflecting the fact that the technical difficulties in making porcelain in Great Britain in the 18th century had been overcome. Occasionally, some of their pieces are impressed with the mark "Lloyd Shelton." The potters Wood and Caldwell also made pearlware models of these lions.

Length 4¾in/12cm $D

Lion & tiger groups

*THE PORCELAIN TIGER AND SERPENT SPILL VASE
group (left) was probably made c.1835–40 by
Samuel Alcock, who produced a wide variety of
animals in porcelain. The Alcock factories, at
Corbridge and Burslem, produced an extensive line
of items, including parian figures and tea wares, and
some of them carry factory marks and pattern
numbers. These animal figures are more difficult
to attribute directly, but some have been known
to carry a small incised model number.*

Height 6¼in/16cm $D

*THOMAS PARR WAS ONE OF A GROUP OF POTTERS BEARING
this name, who worked in Church Street, Burslem,
from 1852 to 1870. Various partnerships can be
traced from here to the William Kent Ltd. factory of
the 20th century. The group of the lion and tiger
(right) is a Thomas Parr type, from c.1860. Kent and
Parr-type pieces are noted for their pale enamels
and the porcelaneous nature of the body.*

Height 8¼in/21cm $D–E

Dogs & children

THE CHILDREN IN THIS PORCELAIN PAIR, DATING from c.1840, are seated on recumbent setters with liver spots. The figures are set on gilt-line bases, with the girls and dogs in slightly different positions. Unlike the majority of groups, these were made of porcelain, the favored medium for manufacturers such as Samuel Alcock and the Rockingham factory in Yorkshire. Another unusual feature is the rectangular bases – most mid-19th century animal groups from Staffordshire are on oval bases. These figures were modeled by hand and by using molds, and they were decorated with overglaze enamel colors.

THERE ARE MANY MID-19TH CENTURY VERSIONS OF children and dogs, some of which are thought to be of the Prince of Wales and the Princess Royal. These groups are more endearing to collectors than the figures of dogs alone, so they usually command a higher price. Larger versions of the children and dog groups could be sold for almost double the price at auction.

Length 4¾in/12cm $C

Various dogs

*P*AIRS OF DOGS AND OTHER ANIMALS, FACING LEFT
to right, are typical of the mid- to late 19th century.
Standard "comforter" spaniels, seated on their
haunches, were produced in large quantities, which
is reflected in their low value. The even-less-valuable
lions and collies in the top row have glass eyes,
illustrating how the format changed c.1900.
*R*ARER FIGURES, FOR EXAMPLE, THE SPANIELS WITH THE
baskets of flowers in their mouths, can be sold at a
higher price. Similarly, the models of "Billy the
Rat Catcher" terriers (bottom left) are highly valued.
Poodles and greyhounds are also popular. The
Saint Bernards (bottom right) command
a high price; they are probably sought by both
Staffordshire collectors and dog breeders.
Height tallest pair 12½in/31.5cm $A–D

Pipe-smoking spaniels

AN AMUSING VARIATION OF THE SUBJECT OF
*dogs is this mid-19th century pair of pipe-smoking
spaniels. While there are thousands of standard
pairs of spaniels, pipe-smoking spaniels are much
rarer, and this is reflected in their value.*

CARE SHOULD BE TAKEN WHEN BUYING SPANIELS OF THIS
*type: the pipes are fragile and often damaged
or missing, having been knocked off. On many pairs,
the pipes are not the original or have been restored
in some way, reducing the value of the figures.
It is better to have a piece with a few flaws than one
that is poorly restored. The almost pristine condition
of this pair is reflected in the price.*

Height 8½in/21.5cm $E

The pipes extend from the
side of the mouth. The ones
on this pair have survived
well, suffering only from
hairline cracks.

Welsh springer spaniel

SOMETIMES KNOWN AS "ON THE SCENT," THIS
*rare Parr-type Welsh springer spaniel c.1860–70 is
poised in a working position. The sport of shooting
has changed since the 19th century, and the
dogs then probably worked differently to their
modern counterparts. In a shooting party, dogs
worked in front. Springers flushed out the game for
the sportsmen. Some dogs pointed at the
game, with their nose, body, and tail in a straight
line, hence the term pointer. Yet others set, or
turned in the direction of, the game, earning the
name setter. Welsh springer spaniels were also used
to retrieve game after it had been shot.*
THE FIGURE SUFFERS FROM A COMMON FLAW ASSOCIATED
*with overglaze enamel decoration. Because
there is no protective glaze, the pieces are
susceptible to damage from blows, and as a result
flaking is common. The value of a figure
is often related to the level of flaking, but the
rarity of the piece is also a factor.*
Length 10in/25cm $D

Spaniels & pups

An adult sits over a recumbent puppy in each of the spaniel groups in this pair. This is a pleasing variation on the spaniel theme: depicting the puppies with the adults and the fact that they are poised on blue enamel bases seem to increase their value. It is amusing to note that the decoration raises a question about the parentage of the puppies, which are marked in black patches rather than the brown ones of the adults. Otherwise, the decoration for these mid-19th century spaniels is standard; they are painted in overglaze enamels.

An interesting feature is the high definition of the animals' hair. This pair was probably produced in a reasonably new mold. Typically, the molds for making figures are used often over a period of time. Eventually, the molds wear, so later pieces lack some of the definition of earlier ones.

Height 8in/20cm $D

Greyhounds

*A PERENNIAL FAVORITE, GREYHOUNDS WERE
produced in a variety of styles. For example, the
greyhound above is holding a hare, and the figure
below has a hole in the base so that it could be
used as a pen holder. These models are only two of
a number made c.1860 and later.*

*THE GREYHOUND WAS A WORKING MAN'S DOG. TO HELP
supplement his pot, the dog was used for poaching
or coursing on common land to catch rabbits and
hares. Workers in the 19th century were poorly
paid, so any food caught in this
way was a welcome addition to
the pantry. This perhaps explains
why there are so many Staffordshire
models of this subject, yet few
made by more exclusive
porcelain manufacturers.*

Height greyhound with hare
7¾in/19.5cm $B–C

Pair of cats

THESE CATS, SITTING ON THEIR HAUNCHES AND *facing left and right, are decorated with liver spots. A red enamel line encircles each base. The pair was probably manufactured in the second half of the 19th century. Dogs were more popular than cats at the time, probably because dogs had been appreciated as household pets for many centuries. Cats, by contrast, were often semiferal, and until the late 19th century, they were still regarded with wariness as a result of medieval superstitions.*

THE RARITY OF GENUINE 19TH-CENTURY FIGURES OF CATS *is reflected in their value. Today, cats are extremely popular, and even later copies of cats in the Staffordshire style are saleable and sometimes appear at auction (but they should not be dated). If you purchase a figure, take care that a later piece is not mistaken for an earlier one.*

Height 4in/10cm $B

Two pug figures

IT IS UNUSUAL TO FIND PUG DOGS DEPICTED
in Staffordshire figures from the mid-19th century.
Their lack of popularity may be because
they were typically the pets of fashionable wealthy
women and were not owned by the type of
people who bought Staffordshire pieces. Figures of
pugs began to appear by the last quarter
of the 19th century, however, and continued
into the 20th century.

THE DOGS IN THIS LATE 19TH-CENTURY PAIR ARE STANDING
on rocky, gilt-lined bases. These pugs may have been
influenced by pieces from the German Meissen
factory, where porcelain models of pugs had been
popular since the mid-18th century. They
are good examples – in the period in which pugs
were made, they were usually not as well
modeled or colored, but were quite crude as,
indeed, are most other Staffordshire figures.

Height 8½in/21.5cm $D

Elephant spills

*THESE CIRCUS ELEPHANTS, DRAPED WITH ORANGE
and green caparisons, or coverings, were produced
c.1860 as spill vases. Elephants are an unusual
subject for most potters and, consequently,
much sought after by collectors. Their relative
rarity may be a reflection of the fact that touring
circuses that owned elephants did not appear in
England until the early 19th century.*

*RARITY IS NOT THE ONLY REASON THAT ELEPHANTS
typically command high prices. The symbol of the
Republican Party is, of course, an elephant, and
Staffordshire figures of this kind are highly
prized for that association. Elephants have been
reproduced in the 20th century, and these
more recent figures are also collectable. If an early
figure is desired, be careful to purchase
one from a reputable dealer – skill is required to
ascertain a piece's date.*

Height 6in/15cm $D

Two pairs of cats

THE BLACK-GLAZED CATS IN THIS PAIR ARE seated with their tails curled around them and bows tied around their necks. They have alert expressions and green glass eyes. Animal groups of this period, c.1900, often have glass eyes – this is nearly always an indication of a late date of manufacture. Not all Staffordshire-type figures were made in the Potteries. These were made by Charles W. McNay and Sons at the Bridgeness Pottery, Bo'ness, Scotland.

Height black cats 12½in/31.5cm $B

THE PAIR OF GINGER KITTENS, MODELED LEFT AND RIGHT, were designed with their mouths open and their forepaws apart from their bodies. Like the cats above, the kittens were produced at a comparatively late date, c.1900 – this reflects the greater popularity that cat subjects enjoyed at the end of the 19th century.

Height kittens 7¾in/19.5cm $B

Bo'ness horses

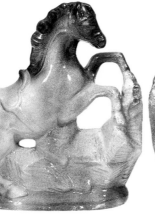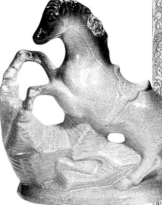

THESE REARING POTTERY HORSES WERE PRODUCED
c.1900 in Bo'ness, Scotland. They were painted
in shades of gray glaze, with hints of brown.
The modeling of the horses is much cruder
than that of typical mid-19th century Staffordshire
groups. The horses' hooves appear clumsily
attached to the rock, giving the impression
that they are galloping through syrup. One
assumption is that the drop in quality reflects the
need to continue to make these figures at
a reasonable price, despite the vastly increased
costs of manufacturing figures at the
beginning of the 20th century.

THE HORSES HAVE A COMPARATIVELY HIGH VALUE,
given that they are late models and the
workmanship is crude. However, there is a
strong collectors' base for this Scottish
work, and of course, horses are as popular
today as they have always been.

Height 6in/15cm $B

Jumbo

A SIMPLE FIGURE of the renowned 19th-century circus elephant Jumbo sits on a round base. Jumbo was a famous beast who toured Great Britain until he became too large to handle. In 1882 he was sold by the Fellows of the Royal Zoological Society in London to the American showman, Phineas T. Barnum, who wanted to take him to the United States.

A PUBLIC OUTCRY LED TO AN APPLICATION FOR A COURT injunction, and Jumbo himself, perhaps reluctant to disappoint his British fans, refused to board the ship. Only cold and hunger eventually drove him aboard the specially adapted Assyrian Queen. His career in the United States was short-lived, however. In 1885 Jumbo was killed when he charged – and derailed – an oncoming train.

THIS FIGURE SHOULD DATE FROM 1882 TO 1885. JUMBO was, presumably, reproduced into the 20th century. Although a simple piece – with little to break off – and of a later period, Jumbo is relatively rare.

Height 6½in/16.5cm **\$B**

Sheep shearer

THIS PORCELAIN FIGURE of a sheep shearer is an unusual agricultural subject for the period, c.1840. It is well modeled, showing high definition and exceptional quality in the gilding and enamel decoration. Due to its rarity, the figure could realize a higher price than expected at auction.

BECAUSE THE SHEEP shearer is made of porcelain, it is likely that it was produced by one of the larger and better-quality Staffordshire manufacturers. For a mid-19th century piece, this figure shows greater attention to detail than usual, and this is also an indication that it was produced by a larger manufacturer. For example, extruded clay was used for the sheep's wool, great care was taken in modeling the facial features, and the decoration was applied more neatly than on standard Staffordshire figures.

Height 6in/15.5cm $B

This lustrous gilding is the result of using a medium of honey or water, not the drab and less durable mercury gilding used later.

Punch & Judy

DESIGNED AS A PAIR, PUNCH AND JUDY ARE SEATED
on goats, facing in. The figures are easy
to identify because they are wearing costumes
associated with the characters.
THE MODELS WERE MADE C.1850 USING ONLY MOLDS,
with the exception of the extruded clay
additions to decorate the goats. These particular
figures represent a rarer type of the standard
genre of people seated on goats. More typically,
the goats were rendered with children –
often the Prince of Wales and the Princess Royal.
Because the children are more common
and appear more frequently at auction, they
generally realize only a sixth of
the value of Punch and Judy, depending
on their size and condition.

Height 6¾in/17cm $C

Death of the Lion Queen

THE ACTRESS ELLEN BRIGHT *was the subject for the figure "Death of the Lion Queen," made c.1850. She was the niece of the circus owner George Wombwell and became a lion queen at the tender age of 16. During her working life, Ellen appeared before Queen Victoria and other notable members of society. In 1850, however, while performing with a caged lion and tiger in Chatham in Kent, England, Ellen was attacked by the tiger, which seized her by the throat and killed her. The affair caused a huge sensation at the time and, ultimately, led to the prohibition of women working with dangerous wild animals, although many circuses continued to have lion kings.*

IN THIS FIGURE, ELLEN IS POSING WITH WHAT APPEARS TO *be a leopard, not a tiger, playfully leaping at her in an unconvincing manner, apparently more ready to lick than bite her. Although this figure is charming, and shows a lion at her side, it is not a very realistic portrayal of Ellen's fate.*

Height 14½in/37cm $C

Llywelyn's Baby

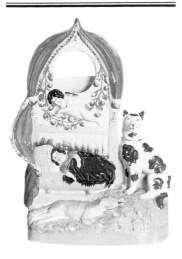

A WATCH-HOLDER GROUP WAS DESIGNED TO
be a safe place to store a pocket watch overnight.
The watch sits in a hollow cup behind the
opening at the top, appearing for all the world
like a clock set in a pottery case.
*T*HIS GROUP OF PRINCE LLYWELYN'S SON AND GELERT
was produced in the mid-19th century. It illustrates
the tragic story of the prince's dog, Gelert.
Llywelyn returned from hunting one day to find his
dog covered in blood. He immediately checked
his son's crib and was horrified to find it empty and
smeared with blood. Enraged, he drove his
sword into Gelert's side, killing him. As the dog let
out a dying howl, the child's cry could be heard
nearby; a mauled wolf was found dead in
the vicinity. Gelert had saved the child's life.
Llywelyn was so upset by his tragic mistake, he
was reputed never to have smiled again.

Height 10½in/26.5cm $B

Lady Isabel Burton

THIS FIGURE OF LADY ISABEL BURTON, MADE
*c.1861, shows her sitting on a camel. She was the
wife of Sir Richard Burton, a well-known
mid-19th century traveler and explorer, and she
accompanied him on several of his travels.*
AT THE TIME, IT WAS EXCEPTIONAL FOR ANY WOMAN TO
*undertake the type of traveling and activities
enjoyed by the couple. One notable exception
was Lady Hester Stanhope, who was unmarried and
had been housekeeper to her uncle William Pitt.
She not only traveled widely, but – scandalously – did
so accompanied only by her doctor. Figures were
made of both women, mounted on camels. They
are usually difficult to tell apart and, indeed,
the presence of Dr. Meryon with Lady Hester is
often the only way of identifying her.*
Height 8in/20.5cm $C

The Tiger Hunter

A MAN SITS ON AN ELEPHANT, WITH A TIGER BY HIS side, in this group known as "The Tiger Hunter."
This is a late example of an elephant group, dated c.1900. The figure looks as though it should have an interesting story attached to it but, as far as is known, no such story has come to light.

PARTICULAR NOTE SHOULD BE TAKEN OF THE RELATIVELY crude molding of the piece for the period. It was probably made from a single mold and so lacks some of the definition and vivacity of pieces by such potters as Sherratt, which were typically made in several stages. Elephant groups, including many 20th-century pieces, are popular at auction.
A group offered at a lower price than the one suggested may be a more recent version of its late 19th-century counterparts.

Height 8½in/21.5cm $C

Equestrian groups

Victor Emmanuel II, king of Sardinia and first king of Italy (left), and Giuseppe Garibaldi (right) feature in this pair of Parr-type equestrian groups. They were modeled c.1861 from an engraving in the Illustrated London News, dated December 29, 1860. Both men are turned in the saddle, and their horses face each other on rocky molded bases, which bear titles. In 1861, Garibaldi was instrumental in bringing Victor Emmanuel to the Italian throne. Garibaldi visited England, where he was a popular figure, in 1864.

Thomas Parr worked in Burslem between 1852 and 1870. This is at the beginning of a period in which a generic grouping of potters made wares that are referred to as "Kent and Parr-type," and it continued until the Kent factory closed in 1962. The work of these potters is identifiable by their use of pale shades of enamels.

Height 15¼in/39cm $D

Crimean War figures

A DEGREE OF RUSSOPHOBIA IN THE MID-19TH
century made figures associated with the Crimean War
popular subjects. Since 1815, Great Britain
had lived through a period of comparative peace, and
public imagination was no doubt fired by military
acts on Russia's southern border. The sultan
of Turkey, Abdul-medjid (left), and the group of three
figures symbolizing Turkey, England, and France
were both made c.1854. The three allied
nations are represented by the sultan, Queen
Victoria, and Napoleon III. The figure of the sultan
is comparatively rare, but figures of British
and French generals abound.

THE DECORATION ON THE FIGURES IS CHARACTERISTIC
of the mid-19th century period. Few colors
were used, and blue was the predominant one. The
figures stand on gilt-lined and gilt-titled bases.

Height sultan 13in/33cm $B
Height allies 10in/25cm $B

Victoria & Albert

ALTHOUGH NOT A MATCHED PAIR, THE FIGURES ARE *of Queen Victoria and Prince Albert. The bodies are made of a porcelaneous material associated with many figures of the 1840s. The pieces are decorated to a comparatively high standard and enriched with gilding. The ermine lining of Queen Victoria's cloak was achieved by applying extruded clay; the same technique was used to fashion foliage on cottage aromatic burners (see p.71).*

QUEEN VICTORIA AND HER CONSORT WERE POPULAR AT THE *beginning of her reign (1837–1901). Her popularity explains why there are, possibly, more models of the royal couple than of any other Staffordshire portrait figures of the mid-19th century. At the time, these were probably comparatively expensive pieces.*

Height Prince Albert 7½in/19cm $A each

Figure of a man & girl

A MAN IN MILITARY uniform holds a bird in one hand while supporting a child with the other in this group. The child is balancing on one leg on a cushion placed on a plinth. She seems to be holding a bunch of grapes over her head – although the man may be holding them instead. This is a difficult group to identify with a subject with certainty. It is a mid-19th century piece and could be an unidentified theatrical group or, perhaps, Prince Albert and the Princess Royal. There are hundreds of figures and groups that cover both royal and theatrical topics, and not all of them have been identified.

THIS GROUP HAS A REASONABLY HIGH DEGREE OF decoration. Although comparatively rare, many portrait groups similar to this one have dropped in value, largely because many collectors now prefer animals.

Height 9¼in/23.5cm $A–B

Actors

*T*HE ACTORS IN THIS RARE FIGURE GROUP OF *c.1852 are probably playing the roles of Romeo and Juliet, but in broadly contemporary dress. This group is similar to the one of the actresses, and sisters, Charlotte and Susan Cushman cast in the same roles (see p.11). While an engraving exists of the two sisters, no evidence has yet come to light to identify the actors on which this particular piece was modeled.*

*I*T WAS COMMON FOR STAFFORDSHIRE POTTERS TO COPY *engravings advertising plays and operas, and as a result, many of these pieces can be somewhat easily identified. An added bonus is that the engravings make it easy to date the groups, particularly if the play had a comparatively short run.*

Height 11¼in/28.5cm $B

Falconer

Despite considerable research, the identity of many Staffordshire figures remains a mystery. This piece, however, has been identified as a falconer with a falcon perched on his hand and game birds in a basket. It could represent a theatrical source, as many other figures do, but it may simply be a falconer.

The mid-19th century piece is richly colored in overglaze enamels, which have survived well. This is particularly evident in the blue dress, which does not display any of the crazing that is often seen in other enamels. The blue enamel will eventually deteriorate, but it seems to stand the test of time far better than any other color.

Figures molded as a block, such as this one, are reasonably durable. When purchasing a piece, however, make sure that any extremities, such as the bird on this figure, have not been restored – these areas are much more susceptible to damage.

Height 10¼in/26cm $A

Signing the Magna Carta

In this mid-19th century figure group, King John is signing the Magna Carta, the basis of the English constitution. This group is a highly colored version of the subject; they were more often sparsely or partially colored.

This model was constructed by the Victorian process of press-molding. To preserve the original, a working mold was created: the front and back pieces of the master mold were pressed together and the hollow filled with liquid plaster of Paris. Each working mold could be used to make several hundred figures without serious deterioration. To make the piece itself, flat sheets of damp clay were laid on the molds, which were pressed together, to be fired and enameled later.

Height 13in/33cm $B

Greenwich Pensioner

THIS UNUSUAL FIGURE, ALSO KNOWN AS "THE
*Amputee," is of a disabled Greenwich pensioner, who
is wearing a tricorn hat, blue jacket, and orange
breeches and sitting on a sled. It was made c.1854.*
THE ROYAL HOSPITAL, GREENWICH, ENGLAND, FIRST RECEIVED
*pensioners, all of whom were retired seamen, in
1705 (the Royal Hospital in Chelsea was for army
pensioners). Although retired, Greenwich
pensioners were still obliged to wear a uniform – the
blue jacket and the hat shown here – and the
hospital had strict rules about conduct, both inside
and outside the grounds. All working seamen
had sixpence a month withheld from their wages to
contribute to the upkeep of the institution.*

Length 3in/7.5cm $C

Cricketers & other figures

A RARE PAIR OF CRICKETERS (TOP LEFT AND right), made c.1865, is among this interesting range of figures. An excellent example of sporting pieces, they are popular collectors' items outside the circle of Staffordshire figure collectors and appeal especially to cricket fans. Their value is about four times greater than the code given below.

*O*THER FIGURES INCLUDE THOSE OF SPANIARDS (center left and right) and the figures of a shepherd and shepherdess (bottom left and right); they have the impressed mark "Lloyd of Shelton." Each of these groups was made c.1845.

Height Cricketers 13¾in/35cm $C each pair

Pugilists

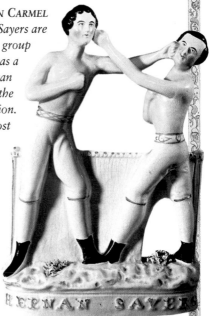

THE PUGILISTS JOHN CARMEL Heenan and Tom Sayers are shown in this group c.1860. Heenan was a celebrated American boxer, Sayers the English champion. They fought the most famous boxing match of the 19th century on April 17, 1860. The fight lasted more than two hours with neither party knocking the other out, and eventually, both men were declared champion.

MOST REMARKABLE WAS THE FACT THAT SAYERS WAS A middleweight boxer, whereas Heenan was not only a heavyweight, but also substantially taller and heavier. In the fourth round, Sayers dislocated his right arm and was only able to survive the rest of the match by using his exceptionally skillful footwork and agility.

IN THE 19TH CENTURY, BOXING WAS A DIFFERENT SPORT FROM its modern counterpart. Men from both the lower and upper classes participated, using bare fists, lightly bound. Points were not awarded, and there was no limit to the number of rounds, hence the unresolved end of the Heenan–Sayers match.

Height 9¼in/23.5cm $C

Highlander spill vase

THIS HIGHLAND *sportsman, with his hound, is well decorated in colored enamels. He is holding a shotgun and has a pheasant at his feet. Behind him is a spill vase modeled as a tree trunk. There are many variations on the theme of Highlanders, and this 19th-century figure is only one example.*

QUEEN VICTORIA AND *Prince Albert had popularized Scotland, choosing to build Balmoral Castle there, and the works of such Scottish novelists as Sir Walter Scott also contributed to this trend. After the last Jacobite rising of 1745, the wearing of tartan was prohibited to weaken the Scottish clan system. However, Victoria and Albert both wore the Stuart tartan during the Queen's reign.*

Height 13in/33cm $B

Swirls of finely painted hair around the liver spots on the dog make the animal's coat look more realistic.

Smith & Collier

A*T FIRST GLANCE, THIS GROUP OF C.1866 MAY*
look like men greeting each other but, in fact, it is a
murder group. In 1866 Staffordshire farmer Thomas
Smith caught William Collier, a neighbor, poaching
on his land. Collier had already used one barrel
from his shotgun to kill rabbits, but used the second
to shoot Smith. He did not kill his victim, so he
bludgeoned Smith to death with the butt of the gun.
Collier was the last man hanged in public at Stafford
jail; the hanging was not a quick one, and it was
decided to execute prisoners in private thereafter.
T*HE MODEL IS NOT STRICTLY TRUE TO THE STORY, AS SMITH*
appears to be standing up to Collier, engaging
in a fight. Doubtless, the fact that the
crime was committed in Staffordshire made it
particularly interesting to potters in the area.

Height 12¾in/32.5cm $B

Rush & Sandford

James B Rush *Emily Sandford*

JAMES BLOOMFIELD RUSH AND EMILY SANDFORD
*are the figures in this pair. Rush owned Potash Farm
(opposite), on which he had taken out a mortgage
from Isaac Jermy. Since Rush was unable to repay
the debt, Jermy foreclosed, and notice was served for
November 30, 1848. On November 28, however,
Rush went to Jermy's house, shot and killed Jermy
and his son, and wounded Jermy's daughter-in-law
and a servant. He conducted his own trial
defense, and Emily Sandford, Rush's lover, gave most
of the evidence that convicted him. The manuscript
she carries probably represents the forgery
she knew Rush had made in an attempt to show
that Jermy had waived the debt.*
THE HIGH VALUE OF THIS PAIR, OF C.1849, REFLECTS
*the relative rarity of these subjects and the
general interest of the story.*
Height Rush 10¼in/26cm $D

Potash Farm

Potash Farm

THIS IS A MID-19TH CENTURY MODEL OF POTASH
*Farm in Norfolk, where James Rush and his lover
Emily Sandford lived and on which the mortgage that
led to murder was secured (see opposite). Models of
celebrated buildings were a popular alternative
to those of the human protagonists, and those with
the title of the house, such as this, are more unusual
than the general models on the market. Stanfield
Hall, where Rush committed the murders, was also
made by Staffordshire potters.*

MODELS THAT WERE NOT PURELY DECORATIVE WERE USED AS
*piggy banks or aromatic burners (to alleviate noxious
odors). The houses are often sparsely colored
in gilt, but they are frequently encrusted with flowers
or extruded clay foliage at the gables.*

Length 9in/23cm $B

Church of St. Roch

THIS MODEL OF THE CHURCH OF ST. ROCH SHOWS
*an unusual building. It has two towers, one on
each side of a central portico, which is surmounted
by a figure of St. Roch, with his staff and dog.
St. Roch is the patron saint of plague victims and is
almost invariably shown with a dog.*

THE CHURCH DOES NOT APPEAR TO HAVE BEEN MODELED
*on an existing building and does not look like a
typically British church, making the subject an
unusual Stafford piece. There is, however, a church
dedicated to St. Roch in Paris, where Napoleon
Bonaparte's troops fired on rebels on October 5,
1795. This mid-19th century example is
probably as large as any model of a building
would ever have been; most of the aromatic burners
and cottages are considerably smaller.*

Height 10in/25cm $A

Military figures

Napoleon Bonaparte (left) was popular
with the British public both during and after his
lifetime, despite waging war against Great Britain
in the late 18th to early 19th centuries. Many
of the diaries of soldiers and sailors refer with
affection to "Boney." There are numerous Napoleon
figures, and many are taken from lithographs
based on works of the great painters.
This mid-19th century figure may have been
modeled from such a source.
Height 9¾in/25cm $B

Nelson (right) was also extremely popular, having
made the ultimate sacrifice for his country in 1805,
and he has lived on in the public imagination
since. In this mid-19th century "Death of Nelson"
group, the admiral is seen at the moment he
was shot, supported by two seamen.
Height 8¾in/22cm $B

Equestrian generals

THOUGHT TO BE A PRUSSIAN GENERAL, THE FIGURE
on the left dates from the time of the Franco-
Prussian war, c.1870. Although only partially
decorated, it nevertheless represents a high level
of decoration for such equestrian figures. The black
enamels show signs of deterioration, a common
occurrence in Victorian portrait figures.

Height 11½in/29cm $A

THE OTHER FIGURE, MADE IN 1857, IS THAT OF GENERAL SIR
Henry Havelock. Sir Henry joined the army shortly
after the Battle of Waterloo, served most of his
career in India and Afghanistan, and was a hero of the
Indian Mutiny, relieving Lucknow in 1857. He was
created a Knight Commander of the Bath as a
consequence, but died shortly afterward. The bases
of such figures are often titled with the general's name,
as many of these figures are similar.

Height 8¾in/22cm $A

King of Prussia

THIS FIGURE OF KING WILLIAM I *of Prussia on horseback was probably made by Samson Smith c.1870. This particular piece has been heavily restored – and not very well. Restoration does not always last indefinitely, and sometimes only for 20 years. The age of this restoration is beginning to show: the restored areas have started to discolor – for example, the neck of the horse has turned yellow.*

OTHER AREAS OF THE FIGURE WERE RESTORED, MAKING *it a good example to study to see where restoration has been done. The King's head has been broken off and reattached to the neck. The base has been damaged and most of the gilt title repainted with gold paint instead of gilt. Other areas of gilt have also been touched up with gold paint, most noticeably the horse's bridle.*

Height 15in/38cm under $A

Fine cracks in glaze, known as crazing, can be caused by shrinkage. Crazing occurs more often in light colors.

Edward VII

MODELED HOLDING HIS HAT, this figure of King Edward VII was made c.1901. It is typical of pieces made at the end of the late 19th century, a period in which Staffordshire manufacturers continued to produce a huge volume of figures. The production of Staffordshire figures began to dwindle in the early 20th century, perhaps because there was no demand for such pieces. For Queen Elizabeth's coronation in 1952 and jubilee in 1977, hundreds of commemorative pieces were produced, but they were printed mugs instead of decorative figures.

THIS FIGURE IS COMPARATIVELY UNUSUAL IN THAT IT IS highly decorated for the period. If end-of-the-century Staffordshire figures have anything in common, it is that they are almost universally sparsely decorated.

Height 12in/30cm $A

Reproductions

Copies of figures made in the 19th century and earlier are still being manufactured today, most notably in the Far East. A well-known factory, William Kent Ltd. of Burslem, continued to manufacture figures that they had earlier produced until 1962. This figure is similar to No. 277, which was featured in their catalog of the mid-1950s. The 20th-century Kent pieces would not necessarily be termed "fake," because – with the exception of World War II – production of these figures had not been interrupted.

Such reproduction figures are seldom sold in specialist Staffordshire figure sales, because they detract from genuine pieces in the sale. These pieces can be bought inexpensively, however, at small auction houses and through the trade.

Height 9in/23cm $A

Glossary

BISCUIT A piece of pottery after the first firing, before it is glazed.
BOCAGE The flower-encrusted bushes or trees seen behind some figures, from the French (thicket).
BODY The mixture of raw materials from which pottery is made.

CRAZING The fine lines or cracks that appear on a glaze, which occurs when the body and the glaze shrink at different rates as they cool after a firing.
CREAMWARE A cream-colored earthenware, or porous pottery, with a clear lead glaze.

ENAMEL A type of smooth paint for decorating ceramics, made of powdered glass, tinted with metallic oxides, and mixed with an oil medium. It is painted on the piece, which is then fired.

FAMILY Literally, a group of potters from the same family.
FIRING The "cooking" of the pottery, glazes, and enamels in a kiln to harden the body or affix the decoration to it.
FLATBACK A figure designed to be seen from the front; the back is unmodeled, or flat.

GILDING Gold paint applied to figures. It was originally applied with an oil, water, or honey medium; later, it was applied with a mercury amalgam.
GLAZE A glass-based coating applied to biscuits as a sealant against moisture.
GROUP A piece consisting of more than one figure.

KILN A specially constructed oven, in which the biscuit and decoration are fired.

OVERGLAZE The process by which glaze is applied over the top of a glazed biscuit piece.

PARR-TYPE Wares in the style of the Parr factory (see p.39).
PEARLWARE A blue tinted glaze applied to the body, possibly in imitation of porcelain, achieved by adding cobalt.
PORCELAIN A thin, hard-fired ware, which is translucent when held to the light and more delicate than pottery. Until the 19th century, only a few manufacturers made it.
PORCELANEOUS A hard-fired fine stone china made in imitation of porcelain, but without the translucent effect.
PRATT-GLAZE A ware colored with glazes similar to ones used by the Pratt family (see p.16).
PRESS-MOLD Where sheets of clay are pressed into two halves of a mold, which are brought together to make a figure.

SALTGLAZE A thin, clear glaze, created when salt is thrown into the kiln and vaporizes.
SLIP MOLD A single mold into which liquid clay is poured in, allowed to dry, then turned out.
SPILL VASE A decorative piece designed to hold spills for lighting fires or pipes.

WOOD-TYPE A ware similar to ones made by the Wood family, but unmarked (see p.21).

Index

Acknowledgments

All pictures courtesy of Christie's South Kensington
except for the following:
Christie's Images: 7, 13–15, 34, 36.
City Museum & Art Gallery, Stoke-on-Trent: 8–9.
City Museum & Art Gallery, Stoke-on-Trent/E.T. Archive: 10.
Garrick Club/E.T. Archive: 11.
Victoria & Albert Museum: 6, 12.
Illustrators: **Lorraine Harrison** (borders), **Debbie Hinks** (endpapers).